Advance praise for *There is Always Light*

Meditative, familiar, evocative. In the tradition of Mary Oliver, Arlene Neal writes about what we all know and need to remember, valuing small things, memories, the every day, family and baseball, flowers and birds, daydreams, passing gas, condiments, Cool Whip and figs, loss, sorrow, regret, and the importance of remembering, writing with *awful fear someday we might forget*, shedding light on all that matters, and like the violets of her first poem, *hushing the violence with steady calm*.

—Scott Owens, Author of *All In*, *Prepositional*, and *Worlds Enough*

Arlene Neal's poetry, as does her person, makes me think of words like humble, honest, and wise. When she first began, reluctantly, showing me her work, I saw poems that had been crafted to their end point, ones from which I learned not just about her world, but my own, ones that made me feel something all the way into my bones. By the time I had seen enough of her work to gauge the consistent quality, I was convinced that Neal is a poet of the finest rank, who shares the richness of a rural and deeply American experience.

—Tim Peeler, Author of *First Season*, *The Birdhouse*, and *Henry River*

Arlene Neal's *There is Always Light* is the mise en scène of a quintessential rural Southern poet. Farm greens, tobacco browns, Goldie hounds, wild violets, sunlit creek minnows turning silver and gold, dark anvil clouds, rusty buckets, gold-tooth grins, cigarette smoke blue and thin, all flicker like frames from a memory-movie set against the white screen of page, each poem holding a complementary hue like a cinematic color palette. One that is eye-full of the chiaroscuro of life's love and loss. One that leaves you with the bittersweet freeze frame of a grandmother and grandson learning to let go of a sunset. One that you will want to re-run. One you won't soon forget.

—Molly Rice, Author of *Forever Eighty-Eights* and *Mill Hill*

Also by Arlene S. Neal

What Came to Me: Collected Columns, 2020, Third Lung Press.

There is Always Light

Poems

Arlene S. Neal

REDHAWK
PUBLICATIONS

Copyright © 2023 Arlene S. Neal

All rights reserved. No part of this publication may be reproduced, distributed, or transmitted in any form or by any means, including photocopying, recording, or other electronic or mechanical methods, without the prior written permission of the publisher, except in the case of brief quotations embodied in critical reviews and certain other noncommercial uses permitted by copyright law. For permission requests, write to the publisher, addressed "Attention: Permissions Coordinator," at the address below.

ISBN: 978-1-959346-17-3

Library of Congress Control Number: 2023943842

Redhawk Publications
Catawba Valley Community College Press
2550 Hwy 70 SE
Hickory NC 28602

https://redhawkpublications.com

Special discounts are available on quantity purchases by corporations, associations, and others. For details, contact the publisher at the address above.

Printed in the United States of America

Third Edition

For my family.

"Just as one candle lights another and can light thousands of other candles, so one heart illuminates another heart and can illuminate thousands of other hearts."

— Leo Tolstoy

Table of Contents

Section One—Back Light

Wild Violets	15
Daybreak	16
Night Ride	17
On the Properties of Anvil Clouds	18
At Seven Years	19
Recollection	20
God Help Me Not to Hate	21
When the Church Burned	22
A Baseball Poem (after Tim Peeler)	23
End of the Season	24
World Series 1966	26
Real Bananas	28
Once When I was Little	29
My Old Hound Lies Down	30
Rain, Late in the Day	31
Sunday Morning Early	32
Nature Knows What to Do	33

Section Two—Day Light

Inch by Inch	37
2 for $3.00	38
All She Needs	39
Fear and Breathing in Walmart	40
Why Do You Laugh When People Pass Gas?	41
Head Noises	42
Conferring the Degree	43
March 14, Eve of the Ides	45
To Answer Your Question...	46
Shifting Condiments	47
Migration	48
Night Fever	49
For the Stewarts	50
In Meetings	52
For the Birds	53
An Afternoon Delight	54
When His Hound Had Puppies	55
On Seeing Adrian's Boyhood Picture	56
I Always Bow My Head...	57
Remembering Them All on the 4th of July	58
To the Old Man at the Store	59
Strange Resort	60
No Place Like Home	61

Section Three—Last Light

50-Year Shingles	65
Let the Granny Roses Run	66
Her Rehab	67
I Would Be Interviewed Late	69
Dividing the Property	70
Friends on Facebook	71
Things Run Out	72
Wayside Wanderers	73
Mama and the Televangelist	74
Evening Light With Liam	75
For Wade	76
Words Failed Me	77
Acknowledgments	79
About the Author	81

Back Light

I am a part of all that I have met.
—Alfred Lord Tennyson

Wild Violets

Botanists explain that wild violets grow
In disturbed earth where things have come apart,
Storm ground eroded or plowed bare and low
Red raw gashes in soil weak from the start.
A violet slips into that sad scene,
Hushes the violence with steady calm:
You all don't need this—this rippet, I mean
Let's just settle down now—then spreads her balm.
Patches wounds, puts torn edges together,
Iodine's medicine where exposed slopes sit
Don't dwell on this—nothing lasts forever,
I'm sure you will hardly remember it.
Hides wild chaos, says *so be it, amen;*
Deep mother roots whisper *never again.*

Daybreak

Mama got up in the dark
just as the chickens stirred.
Unlike them, she kept quiet
except for the squeak
of cabinet door opened
or scrape of frying pan
across cold wood stove.
She watched first glow
behind the barn grow gold
and studied the cow's dark shape,
stretch-necked cropping off
dewy grass and broom straw stubble
as if day nor night mattered.
She scooped flour for biscuits
quiet as snow sifting
and moved in dim half-light,
her day's small peace—
no desire to spoil the dawn with artificial light.

Night Ride

I ride my bike on a whippoorwill night
fast along the fence where cool creek air
parts my hair with sweet scents of honeysuckle
and fresh mowed hay. Black trees loom and
hazy stars hang in new moon darkness over fields.
I pedal harder and pass unseen snakes,
quick before they think of me!
Frogs peep down around the creek banks
while cicadas chirp and clatter all together.
They say, Faster! Faster! My tires sizzle,
I squint my eyes against the gnat cloud
and hold my breath 'til they're behind me.
An owl's dark body swoops overhead
and disappears without a shadow.
Kitchen light streams across the front yard,
where I leap down and bound four steps in two
dodging porch light moths.
My front wheel still spins
when I sit down for supper.

On the Properties of Anvil Clouds

Scientists say storms are generated by the convergence
of contrasting air masses, hot against cold, which cause
positive & negative charges within the atmosphere,
exactly true back then when thunder rumbled
and we ran terrified by their awful words
in dark upper-level disturbances.
By god you—no-you-won't—
well I'll be damned if—
GET OUT! If by chance
the cloud burst before
we found cover,
hailstones hard,
would pound us
huddled in the rain.
But most of all we feared
lightning strikes, searing jolts,
charges we weren't made to hold,
the current burning through our bare feet,
welding us to the ground from which we came,
a deep foundation forged on dark anvil clouds.

At Seven Years

I ran loose and leggy in weeds
and fields, my hound ahead.
On a dim fall evening near
suppertime, I rested
in the hay shed with him.
Rain fell, tapping the tin roof
soft and steady and I felt
his velvet ears in the stillness,
saw my breath matched his.
Porch light proved nightfall
and I heard my name called,
telling me to return, making
that cruel announcement
You can't stay out there forever.

Recollection

Fried squash with cornbread
New potatoes and blackberry dumplings
sweet garden corn waist high.
The man on the red tractor
Tipped his cap to his true love,
She shooed off foolishness
and kept picking peas
into her old rusty bucket.

God help me not to hate

my Sunday School teacher
the way she nods and smiles
at the nice girls who live
in brick homes and wear
pink pearl nail polish and wear
pleated skirts and new shoes
I sit on both my hands
so she won't see my black nails
and fingers stained yellow
from working in tobacco
I don't raise my hand because
of that and she talks mean to me
in front of the nice girls
so I just stare at the picture
of Jesus behind her head
He is looking down at a lamb
in his arms smiling at it
Teacher asks if we know
who Jesus is I don't raise my
hand but I know the answer
He's everything she ain't.

When the Church Burned

It started with that ice pick stab
of lightning knocking the steeple
in pieces across a gravel parking lot.
Old attic dust and wooden trusses,
white heated far beyond their ability
to rest in peace over the sanctuary,
sent flames across the roof and
down walls in fire fingers peeling paint,
heat streaks scorching, roaring for more,
blistering wooden window frames,
blowing out stained-glass shards as
rainbow confetti on the dry lawn.
Hymnals offered pulp pages to the fire,
curled them song after numbered song,
oak pews struck to flame like a revival.
A fireman devout ran to extinguish
the altar ablaze but stopped when told
to let it burn while souls gathered,
huddled under an angry black sky of
storm clouds, smoke steam water and fire,
in awe of what is called an act of God.

A Baseball Poem
(*After Tim Peeler*)

To write baseball poems
Is really the yearning to see
Daddy standing beside his old green Chevy truck
that he painted himself, posing for a picture
before the game, in a community ball uniform
Mama washed, even ironed out its wrinkles.
After all his alcohol acting out she could be proud of this—
I saw it in her eyes, a rare thing. Let's get a picture she said,
and he scowled but grinned a little.
Game time I heard crowd comments around me:
Mighty swing. Homerun record. Cracked bats.
Lost balls never found. Scared pitchers.
What he coulda done before the War. Shell shock.
I picked up a splinter of a bat before we left,
wind blew stinging sand across that red dirt field empty.
I am in awe of the power to split ash,
in dread of another man sittin'
slumped in the porch swing by suppertime,
crying as waves of Philippine dreams
wash over him reciting, remembering,
Mighty Casey at the bat.

End of the Season

Wally stands squints into the sun
cap pulled low against the glare
late in this day, waits for the pitch.
I stretch my fingers wide inside the glove,
pound the ball hard against my palm,
precious leather, familiar old smell.
Daddy and uncles watch across the yard.
Skinny legs trembly, I turn right
raise my arms, a new sweat scent
a hint, warning of that hateful place
I dread to go, the end of life as I know it—
where the way forks, us growing apart.
There's anger in my arm now,
my fingers find the right places,
fingertips on stitches pressing hard.
I could pitch blind I think.
Wally squats, opens his glove,
open shut open shut, butterfly wings.
Ready, he says, and I am
brain and body and ball, all one motion
one current released. It flies away
then curves in, wafts up then falls
slight as a corn leaf lifted
up and down on a breeze.
Wally takes the jolt—a thud—
his thin glove suffers a blow

his wrinkled brow says so.
Uncle Dewey turns to spit,
flashes his gold tooth grin,
raises his eyebrows at my daddy.
Damn! he says,
that's purdy good—
for a girl!

World Series 1966

Daddy lay still on the couch,
cigarette smoke blue and thin
in television light, half-way
watching Walter Kronkite,
forgetting the Dodgers and
Drysdale and Koufax,
drifting into his Philippine dreams,
when the boy came that night.

We left without speaking, not
to stir the sleeping slugger,
Mama's hands in dishwater
never lifted to wave, staring
down my fishnet hose, flimsy
and cold in late October air
where Jade East drifts heavy,
blonde breath short and white.

I tugged my wool jumper down,
the one like Twiggy's, trying hard
to reach my knees but hopeless
in the bucket seat too far too deep.
I didn't know him or his friends
from Up North, his hair ruffled
like John Lennon's partly covering
pimples red and raw pitiful clawed.

At the drive-in movie, he talked
of big schools, God being dead,
weed, acid music, and the Stupid War,
biting his nails between topics,
but he was free enough not to
wear socks in winter and talk
even when no one listened, so
I startled when he showed intentions.

I shut my eyes and ears ashamed
hating his breath and clumsy hands,
sick of the war and freaks and beaded
potheads and dishonest politicians,
all there in fogged up windows. But,
to this day, try as I might, I really
cannot remember what the movie
was about, or who won that game.

Real Bananas

Daddy told me that in the Philippines
real bananas ripen on the trees
and taste much better than ours.
Back home, the green ones
turned yellow did not taste the same
as before the war, like other things too,
And I think he had a hard time with that,
with coming back to act like everything
felt fine and tasted good when really
war ruined him for what he came back to
and he never stopped running from
what he knew to be so terribly real.

Once when I was little

In the middle of hot July,
when grass scorched and
corn burned in the field,
I leaned on my hoe and
dug my toes deep in red dirt,
closed my eyes to piercing sun
and thought of snow, of sleet
falling, prickly on my skin,
of icicles and and crisp air,
hard things frozen, still gray sky
suspended in hushed heavens
to fend off that hot melting—
the end of earth where everything
flames as I learned is supposed
to happen. I heard that people freezing
think that they're burning up, and
I wondered if I burned to death
out there in the field, would I feel
like I was freezing?

My Old Hound Lies Down

Oh, how I wanted one
Wanted that fluffy circus dog
With rhinestone collar and cute tutu
To bounce jump through flame hoops
To make people laugh, clap in glee,
my satin and sequins sparkly,
I bow low, Goldie under my arm
That beautiful dog knows the ropes.

But my old hound lies down
dreads that red hula hoop,
crimped one pulled from the trash,
unusable for hips, but good for tricks.
He teeters through at ground level
With a push on his boney rump,
feeble years untrainable.
I think of him, long gone,
his eyes teaching me more
than applause of approval
when all these hoops loom ahead
that I am loathe to leap,
trembling, afraid of the fire.

Rain, Late in the Day

Before the barn door
rain drips from the roof
where he sits on overturned bucket,
elbows on knees, leans forward,
gnarled hands dangle useless.
Rain pecks the tin roof but
turns staccato drummer as
fields disappear in walls of water.
He leans back against the door frame,
eyes closed, breathes damp hay, dust.
Flies settle still on harness leather.
This rain brings respite, work suspended,
not to begin again this late in the day.
The kitchen window glows.
Hard rain has come before and will again
Like fogs and storms, snow showers and sleet,
but he's made peace with this rain,
takes its comfort, at ease in the evening.

Sunday Morning Early

I'm stuck with re-runs, ever re-runs
But few new shows bear the truth
Like the old, flesh and blood repository
Of scenes re-playing again and again.
The inebriated sings Amen to the beach
And back. A naval hero terrified at night
Dreams of war, screams unholy terror,
Plows plants plays fights teases
Reaps sleeps smokes and smokes,
Chronic cough in the night, lungs fight
A great heart wild and frail fails and fails
Falls to kitchen floor not one heartbeat more
On that Sunday early in spring home free,
Leaving *What If* the epitaph and
I'm left with re-runs, only re-runs
With awful fear someday I might forget,
Unmoored, might not remember all this.

Nature Knows What to Do

When hands wring and fret nervous
over his old farm fallen into ruin.
He could not manage it, you know,
Daughter murmurs half to herself,
That rusty roof, tin pieces missing.
But nature sends vines, green and
tender twining up loose boards
never nailed back to close the gap,
tells swallows to keep company
in eaves, on beams, with
sparrows and mourning dove
in their evening wake of field songs.
Spiders web shrouds for shovel and hoe
while black-eyed mice clean out
the last of old corn and oats.
Nature knows when wind
will usher it down and then
send wild rose runners to
conceal the collapse, as if in apology—
Please excuse the mess—
while her borers return the barn wood
to earth, as if it never were.

Day Light

There is always light. If only we're brave enough to see it. If only we're brave enough to be it.

–Amanda Gorman

Inch by Inch

An inch is such a small thing
Set by the width of a thumb
Or three barley corn kernels
Set end to end by the ancients.
It is a worm, a ribbon width
Pants hem or paper clip
Three a credit card's swipe
Six measure restroom tiles
Nine make a standard dinner plate
Twelve, serious snow here in south
(TV says thirty-six up in Boston)
It rhymes with flinch, cinch, pinch
And as I am substandard Southern
Also bench, wrench, trench.
I may come with an inch of my life
But that still means hope
As I inch backwards,
He on the other hand,
Won't budge an inch
But if I give him one
He will take a mile.

2 for $3.00

I remember that frazzled chicken
Whose gene selected breast
Gave this great filleted white meat
For my biscuit hot and buttery
I bow my head to her suffering
In the cramped coup of floundering
Feathered meals aboard the truck
Deceive myself that she did not
See the green fields through slats
Of cages rattling off to slaughter
Better she never knew the world
Of beetles and flies and worms
Never knew a butterfly chase
But only beaks and beady eyes
Of her peers, hearts beat hard
Breast to breast pressed against hers
Necks strained in useless fight or flight
Neither matter, the appetite of the world
Awaits.

All She Needs

A woman stands behind me
at the grocery store checkout,
and not to be nosy, but I do
discreetly look into her cart:
ten large tubs of Cool Whip
to stock up she tells us all.
News last night mentioned
a shortage, so she creates
one, of course, because
after all, at the end of the world
there must be Cool Whip.

Fear and Breathing in Walmart

A woman coughed hard in Walmart.

All eyes down her aisle

pinned her like a specimen

to study her symptoms.

They hold their breath

to run the checklist:

Feverish? Sweating? Congested?

Like a broken jar of pickles,

They skirt around her with

glaring judgements, outright sneers.

What's wrong with you?

Where is your mask?

Stay home if you are sick!

You're what's wrong with America!

She clutches her coat collar,

pushes her cart to checkout

and says to herself:

I hate it when people

wear perfume in public.

Don't they know some of us

are allergic?

Why do you laugh when people pass gas?

Is it the absurdity of fumy bodies full of fermentation
housing lofty ideas? Is it the sound itself?
As a mustard dispenser almost empty splatters
like flatulence across a hot dog with chili?
Is it the ridiculousness of your own gassy guts,
your own breaking wind, anal language,
planned or unplanned, that makes you laugh
because you know the passage like 6th grade boys of old,
hand cupped armpits pumping compressed air hysterical?
Do you laugh to deny the truth we're all wind bags?
The old don't care to conceal the emissions anymore,
having held back their entire lives, sphincters sad, stretched.
Unrestrained little kids delight to disgust with fumes
with the power to evoke eew! among the mature,
a mere mention of poot brings them to tears,
like the two in the back seat laughing so hard
they snort when one points to the bank
and cries, *Look! Wells Fartgo!* Who started this!
Some caveman? Who held out his hand to his cave kid
and said *pull my finger?* Still, something happens there
when windy guts sound and strike the funny bone.
I don't understand. Why do we laugh when people pass gas?

Head Noises

Here I lie to watch
the ceiling sky and
wait for the night ether,
let the keyboard cool,
and red burners darken cold.
Let papers stop rustling
and hush the loud voices
that tell me things
over and over
and over.

But above all the voices
that I most dread,
is the chiding one
inside my head.

Conferring the Degree

He slipped into the gym late after work
with a grocery store rose bouquet,
stuck it beneath his seat, eased down
rubbed his knees and leaned back,
hands worrying his wedding ring.
Seemed odd not to sit with her now
in the multitude of bobbing mortarboards
black gowns, gold cords, dignitaries
she'd stand out he knew—high honors,
precious gold tassel, head high chin up.
He tried not to think about that look,
the one she gave him too many times
but it's there like a worn wallet picture.
He'd stacked wood chest high in the shed
white oak, all of it, dried out, hot burning,
winter heat stacked ready for the worst.
Come see it, he says, expects her smile.
I've got a paper to write she snaps.

On a Saturday night he tried to take her
out to eat—daring to stir up desire
or at least obligation—but she shrugged,
spread papers out on the table and
huffed without looking his way.

You take the kids and go. I can't
project's due Monday. So, he stayed,
fed the kids cereal, put them to bed
watched TV 'til one, slept on the couch,
lulled under by slow talk show chatter.
Three years of this. Now Graduation Day--
and he can't quite believe this is the end.

March 14, Eve of the Ides

Driving the mill road this morning
I see him again, ready for me,
this white-whiskered lab half-lunges
from a safe distance in his yard, turns
slow stiff legged toward the porch,
his intimidation duty done.
Five miles on and then Steve,
silver stubble under his helmet
revs his Harley loud and long
for all of us trapped at the light.
He eases through the intersection
his leather jacket mellow, soft from age
patched, comfortable second skin
like old dog velvet circling, circling,
before lying down to sleep in the sun.

To Answer Your Question, No, the Circle Will Not Be Unbroken

I loved that close couple in our young circle

His Johnny to her June, true love and all,

who did the same as the rest—marry, make babies

collect stuff, observe seasons and work at life.

The ties that bind grew thin when finances failed,

money and irresponsibility dissected relations.

They fought wild like bobcats over territory

but on summer nights soft in the mountains

they tried to repair but had the wrong lyrics

and danced to music they hated because

it was expected that they suffer together alone.

When it ended, they did awkward things apart

nothing left to salvage, just scorched field, but

when she called him about the taxes that day

I wondered to myself—

when he heard her voice

did it still make him smile?

Shifting Condiments

Back home we only had mayonnaise and mustard
to begin with before Mama went to the factory.
With her check she could buy frozen French fries,
so we needed catsup like they had at Al's Diner
and like on TV, every happy family had catsup.
(Well, we did have Texas Pete too but only
because Daddy burned his taste buds off.)
But my kids were privileged. They started out
with all three—Duke's and French's and Heinz.
Oh, I never dreamed of this day arriving
with these now grownups coming home
with their uncommon condiments.
It started with a suggestion that I should buy
brown mustard (like yellow is not enough?)
Dijon, aioli, avocado mayo, gremolata, horseradish,
sriracha, picante, oh the gates of hell
could not get things hot enough for them.
Now my refrigerator door is filled with
Strange sauces, some green—on purpose!
But sometimes by myself I'll take a saltine
dab some Dukes on it and closed-eyes savor
the favor of home, of that jar of yellow mustard
and Daddy yelling from the yard
Y'all come on out here
bring the weinies,
I got this fire going!

Migration

By June, goldfinches leave me
Black, yellow, white taken flight
To wherever it is they go
I don't ever know.
But they will return one day
in drab olive and gray
dull coats to blend with
winter birds unnoticed.
They feed, fight, fly
only soon to leave again,
like a loved one home
from a long stay away.
My how you've changed!
So good to have you here!
But you won't stick around.
You'll go. I just know.

Night Fever

I'm no different from the others,
women who walked ahead
clutching babies to their bosom.
They saw consumption waste away
dimples of warm cheeks turned cold.
I hold this still child on my lap and
I'm no different from the forgotten,
the woman who laid her lanky boy
in a lonely dry grave along a wild trail,
prayed wolves not find him, never to return.
No different from those who watched polio
take prancing bare feet and warm breath away.
No different from her who gazed in grief
while curly hair fell from her cancer child.
Here I sit rocking, no different at all,
Except this brown-haired boy
Damp head against my chest
Is sleeping.

For the Stewarts

Peripheral vision comes in handy
where without full stare
I study the family before me
waiting for service.
This strawberry blonde boy haloed
by neon bar glow looks light enough
to fly, tee shirt falling off slim shoulders,
cargo shorts too rough for stick legs.
A rear window decal family:
Father, mother, sister, brother.
Sit up Stewart, dad hisses,
laces his fingers, thumbs under chin,
glares, bounces tan legs under the table,
white running shoes spotless.
He orders for Stewart—mom corrects:
No soda, they said he can't have sugar.
Stewart watches the fish mobile overhead,
a swarming school under air vent.
Mom and sister go into their phones
highlighted hair hides any expression.

There is Always Light

A wine glass stem bends light
casts a wall spectrum across beach art,
Stewart stares at the spectacle.
Beer arrives for parents, soda for sister,
water for Stewart who doesn't open the straw.
Stewart! Dad rumbles low. *Stewart!* Louder
then grabs, squeezes a thin hand hard.
People look over, he releases, looks away,
limes his beer, sips like nothing happened.
Sister flips her hair, elbows Stewart,
who returns from somewhere over that rainbow,
gives her a crooked smile made of light
that passes through every clear space,
that makes shadows behind
the dense places where he cannot go.
Remember to sit up, he tells himself.

In Meetings

When a dead horse
beaten beyond recognition
bleeds numbing Novocaine
and a powerless PowerPoint voice
reads aloud what I have read,
I slip away to the creek for ferns,
mossy rocks, minnows and
to listen to the trickle. I wait
for Odonata, the toothed dragonfly.
It glitters green, flashes iridescent
hovers humming weightless.
I will it to land on my pen poised
for notes if I should return.
Fierce teeth, head of eyes
turns clockwise to look at me,
Any questions?

For the Birds

Robin on stick legs body brown and rust
Stands head-cocked in winter's dead grass
Worms too deep today lie cold and silent
Ice coats our branches, bends our trees
Gives us brittle twigs against a lead sky—
Robin! Fly!

Cowbirds sweep down from oak trees
Greedy for birdseed in furious feed
Turn lawn to shiny black bobbing sea
Some chemistry sends them airborne
As one in fluid unity of flight grace
These common careless birds leave
Their only fault pure numbers.

Purple grackle at the window
Cocks his iridescent head
Yellow eye keen in stark regard
Of his glass reflection before me
He lifts wide wings to field to pasture
I pour my mug and sit sad that he left
Without feeding and did not stay the day
I wonder what to do and I envy his agenda.

An Afternoon Delight

Friend of weak palate
grimaces in disgust
shivers, turns away
when I break the brown skin
and pull apart soft red entrails
full of juicy quivering flesh.
I tell her ancients knew this fig
that succored armies, that
celebrated victories.
Forget the apple—Eve gave Adam
an irresistible fig, some say.
Forget the laurel wreathes,
Olympians won fig prizes too.
Why thousands of years
of history are in this treat!
She looks back at me when
I chomp the fig whole and
with juice dribbled chin, say
Look, you don't know what you're missing!

When his hound had puppies

Daddy showed me squirming milk-bellied babies,
miniatures of their mama. He stood hands on hips gazing
into that corn crib nursery. *Now some mama dogs will eat
their pups* he mumbled, casual as it might rain today.
All hours of the day I ran to see if the puppies survived,
afraid mama teeth might kill. But she endured her young
'til her teats hung low, thin and dry.
Another life later I thought of that dog and what Daddy said,
when a troubled girl in class one day dropped her pencil and
blurted out *My mama left me when I was a baby and never
came back.* And then when she boarded a fieldtrip bus
she laughed: *I got my lip gloss and my happy pills!* She kept
depression demons at bay.
I will always wonder about that girl's mama,
wonder if she left because she knew something
knew she didn't trust herself not to eat her young.

On Seeing Adrian's Boyhood Picture

His hands speak as he stands only a moment,
large heart proud under wool sweater
a young body unaware of pain changes,
oceans away, time appointed, separated.
Left hand pocketed firm, he's guarded,
right hangs loose in late sun, a gate open
almost trusting, as a child early on can be.
Such soft clay in other hands—
ones that ruffled those curls
and tended fevers and hoisted
him upon stout shoulders
and cruel ones in crying times
too harsh for tender limbs
for a child all hands and heart,
too soon gone from them.

I always bow my head in that sacred silence

when grief grips throat and tongue in
profound quiet. That night, the poet
paused mid-stream, picked his way
across mossy stones, word to word
to word to trembling word, to the falls
where he hung suspended on the precipice
of pain, his voice caught on recollection
snagged just below the flow of phrases,
hanging only by his fingertips pressed
hard into the page. We waited, willed
him back across the water unaware that
the room filled with each our own solitary
pools of sorrow all still reflecting
what seemed our father's face.

Remembering Them All on the 4th of July

They did not plan to leave forever,
only a trip to store or church,
school or work. They would be back.
See you later, we're going to the parade.
They did not think to say I won't be back
and you will live the rest of your lives
without me.
No, far from it—they thought happiness
bands, clowns, kids' laughter candy thrown,
beauty queens on sports cars floats fire trucks
dance troops Boy Scouts and old soldiers, flags.
Not bullet barrage, not run for your lives
and chaos and bloody shoes left on the street,
not that lone abandoned baby stroller
overturned in the terror.

To the Old Man at the Store

What is the one great sorrow,
the driving regret remaining?
Yet nothing can be done now
after all these years gone away.
Skin over splinters still lodged,
untouchable, painful with pressure.
Regret is a medallion on a string
rubbed smooth with worry,
a lip bitten so long and hard the
blood vessels learn a new path.
What broken branch survives,
half-hanging from the tree
ruined but alive?

Strange Resort

I find things strange here at the beach resort
seven floors up in a high rise among high rises
where no one hangs towels from the balcony rails,
no one lugs cardboard boxes of Spam and bread
and mayonnaise, sardines and Little Debbie cakes
to camp out in the rented room far from home.
No one calls out across the way at dawn
Hey y'all, anything bitin' last night? No one smokes
and flicks the butts onto the sandy grass below.
I saw no one bleary-eyed with beer sing old songs
in tears as the ocean pounds, water that surely
flows all the way back to the Philippines
washing up ghosts in the surf, like a dark-skinned boy
holding out his hand for help—
Seagulls call out plain as day—why why why?
No one makes eye contact, no one remembers
the guns like the boom of waves that fall
to the ocean floor, dragged back out to return,
no will of their own where forces far stronger rule.
No one here has a red cooler full of dead men's faces
nor the sweet relief to make them go away.

No Place Like Home

If I had seen myself
in Dorothy's crystal ball,
calling your name
walking the yard wondering
what happened to you,
I could have paid more attention,
worked harder to keep you close
to make you feel protected,
but things went another way.
You didn't get the thing
you needed, and no house
fell on your worst fears.
No heel clicks have brought
you back to me.

Last Light

I have so much of you in my heart.
— John Keats

50-Year Shingles

Days of hurricane rains bring seeping stains,
Evidence of angry elements upper hand to ruin
Roof and upstairs ceiling bleeding damp gray,
Testament to our aging abode. So, he says,
Something must be done. He knows a man.
The roofing rep spreads open his sales case,
Blue-grays, grainy greens, and slate samples
I try to visualize how it will be up there—
Now this one here, he hesitates, *it does*
Cost a little more, but you two won't ever
Need worry again. Guaranteed 50 years.
We run the numbers in our heads, his,
The cost of shingles, mine, the shingle years
Beyond my own. Slate slabs sealing
Our residence reside up there now
worry-free weather protectors,
but when I drive home tired
Turning in at evening, they stare, note
My disrepair and coming numbered day,
One they will oversee.

Let the granny roses run

Up weathered boards, windows
Climb the chimney stones send
Old timey rose scent the shortest
Road to memories transporting
Faded aprons, braids, blue veiny hands
and apple peelings in dishpans
Ban those proper American Beauties
Knock Outs and modern hybrids
Temperamental, fungus prone be gone!
Make peace with the wild roses
Thorny, only once a year appearing
Merely asking for summer rain
Sun, space to run and roots deep
A promise to be there next year.

Her Rehab

A doctor's voice too sweet to trust
Or even begin to believe croons
You'll be so proud of her!
Resentment wrings my heart dry
Aching over the trouble we're in,
The end of things, of ways set.
Double doors swoosh open on
Stainless steel lifts and pulleys
Wheelchairs, rolling carts askew
Floor puzzles and big red balls.
She sits waiting, frizzy-haired
Beyond embarrassment without
Makeup or lipstick or earrings.
I know she's playing along
Anything to get out of here,
PT lady coaxes the child
Honey, show her what you can do
Those hands, the same ones I saw
Throw a hay bale like Daddy
That cradled my head in her lap
Tucked curls behind my ears
While preacher droned on and on
That screwed lids on scalded jars
And axed the rooster for Sunday
That would have taken a nail in palm
And bled for me—

Those hands grip the walker
I do not breathe
She lifts a weight-bearing
Trembling will to out-run this,
A newborn unfolding stiff limbs.
Sneakers someone else tied step one tile
Then with slight shuffle another
White coats titter silly exclamations
Her flint gray eyes set on me
Sly half-smiling mocking it all,
Throws her head back like
Beauty on a parade float
Oh, yes, look how well I'm doing
But don't you dare be proud of it.

I Would Be Interviewed Late

When I enter they are already there
across the massive mahogany table,
shuffling important papers, waving be seated
before the altar built for the god of conference.
I see my face down in the dark polished slab,
and wonder at the day its mighty tree fell.
I remember sawdust settled on Daddy's shoulders.
Git back, he yells, *what are you doin' here?*
That blade cut a man clean in two one time.
I ease into the chair where they walk around,
wonder if I'm sound, arms spread to measure
my girth, feel my gnarls, drill to count my rings.
Then I see it on the conference walls
above their heads where the wallpaper peels,
days coming when branches stripped bare scrape
against the empty windows of this place,
ancient oaks uprooted, heedless of date and agenda.
What will you do? they ask. Maybe stand while I can
save some out of the sawmill, grow roots against the day.
They eye each other. That will be all.
Stiff-limbed I rise to leave under a fog canopy of gray,
tremble with fear that at the first cut
they find my heartwood rotten.

Dividing the Property

Our city-bred surveyor in clean boots
wide-stepped our broom straw field and
woods looking for boundary markers.
Law says we must have him here,
so we can say what's hers, his, and mine,
as though we could really own the land.
Grandpa's oak that guards the spring
with roots deeper than this century,
has witnessed deals long before ours.
Surveyor spoke in clipped phrases
bitten off crisp like ice breaking.
His face froze, as if slapped, when I looked
over his shoulder to where Grandpa's cherry tree
once grew, and teased him:
Y'ain't frum'round here are yuh? I laughed
and explained the context of my question,
but he looked uneasy and did not see the humor,
the joke in all this, the eons of human affairs,
people scratching lines on the earth calling it theirs.

Friends on Facebook

High school long past held us
in chemistry lab of flaming sulfur
after Chaucer's April heat before
P.E. found us perspiring,
then lost in World Civilization.
We time travelers separated by
the turn of our tassels, now arrive,
assemble our fragmented forty
short alumni years: online grannies,
divorcees, retirees, all free, Facebook open.
We pass notes in comment boxes, put
heart emojis to our posts, gather
during our recesses to open online albums,
to search for the girls we knew then and now,
knowing full-well we hide there behind screens,
voices silent, aging, fading, fearing the coming
final exam and long overdue books never returned.

Things Run Out

I buy your favorite coffee
but it will run out again and
then again, a consumable,
the thing that always runs out.
I remember my daddy
on the day we drove past
the Chevy dealership
when I was sixteen with a
brand new driver's license.
He pushed his ball cap back
pointed to a new Nova and
said, *I'd let y'all pick out
which one you want—any of 'em
if I owned this place.* I smiled
and he added—*and a gas pump
that'd never run out.* He chuckled
and coughed and coughed hard.
On a March morning he gasped
his last, a life of hard days run out.
Now I sip this coffee with you
each morning a cup raised to toast
what I know will in the end run out.

Wayside Wanderers

Every June they appear and if flowers
can be lonesome, I think they are.
Old timey orange daylilies too common,
left behind by hybrids with names like
Persian Market & Rosy Scenario pitched
Charming! Gorgeous! Striking! Glorious!
The old ones exiled from farmyards
once lived plain where chickens scratched
and poor dirt flower beds bathed in
gray wash water from dish pans or
storm rain pounding hard. Sometimes
I think they are homesick for that old life
gone away. Now they are scattered
on roadsides, down weedy creek banks
like grannies gone away too soon.
Offspring bloom where they can
if only for one day.

Mama and the Televangelist

Wee hours of the morning when she could not sleep
TV preacher in silky blue suit speaks straight to her,
Comforts her with words that she wants to believe:
"God knows you're lonely."
Walt gone years back, everybody dying on this red ridge
I need to move from here.
"God wants you to partner, plant your seed of prosperity."
No, not for me, for my children.
"God knows you have pain."
Yes, and I will stay away from hospitals even if I hurt.
"God can and will heal you."
If only that wind would quit blowing so cold.
She pulls a blanket up around her neck
God, if only I could see the way.
"We walk by faith and not by sight."
If only I had the faith, if only my seed were big
enough to get the blessing.

Evening Light with Liam

We walk hand in hand to the house
late summer evening air cool
after our hard work in garden rows.
The sun hangs burning orange
over soft Blue Ridges, melting into
lavender cream clouds.
Grandson points to the panorama
sky drama turning down the day.
It's going away, isn't it, he says.
We face the west to wait for it,
last light show when sun slips away.
He kneels to rub some itchy spot
I cry, oh, look there it goes—
He pops up, then sighs, bites his lip
in disappointment at dark mountains
rimmed in afterglow, night stage set.
He leans in and I hug him close,
That's the way it is, I say, you see,
the closer to the end, the faster things
go and lace his fingers firm in mine.

For Wade

If I had known the years
were set to slip so quickly
through my grasping fingers,
I would have held you longer
on the porch while the sun slid
down behind our blue ridges.
I would have watched you closer,
felt your curly hair soft
and studied those stout legs
dangling from the swing.
I could have pushed you higher.
If I had known, I would
have pulled the wagon
one more time around the yard.
It wasn't hard but I
didn't know that then.
I would have listened closer
to your truck sounds
in the sandpile that the years
have washed away.

Words Failed Me

The day my poems were due
to the publisher for a last chance
get something out there before
you die and for the kids thing,
I sat looking at the black
under my ragged fingernails,
that soot covered every surface
of my brother's burned home
where he died in his hoarder
house of bags and boxes and
Marine Corps uniforms and dog tags
and Christmas decorations melted
into a mass of wire and plastic of
Season's Greetings and sooty tinsel
and lighter fluid, so much lighter fluid.
I stood where he fell beside the
washing machine never fixed
smoke inhalation a mercy before
the burning burning burning.
Do you know a burned body
cannot be embalmed? —it leaks
and will soil a satin casket they say.
I chose not to see him, to remember
curly hair, hazel eyes, handsome at 64,
And yes, we still loved him.
Lejeune's chemicals across his
blood brain barrier took him far away

never understanding what happened
to him and thirty others in the unit
all sent home insane, brains afire
broken men discarded in the cover up,
water unfit to drink with 70 toxins
from that well of dry cleaner fluid and
God only knows what else coursed his
body and what damage came to a
brain bright with art and mechanics.
There will be words and more words
in time when I go back to the creek
and he is with me catching minnows
sunlight glitter in his sandy hair.
Look, he says, *how the light turns
them silver and gold,* and the creek
murmurs on over mossy stones and
wind lifts leaves high in our old oak.
We sit still on the rocks listening
waiting for all we cannot yet see.

Acknowledgments:

Tim Peeler, I first heard the crack of the poetry bat from you. Thank you for your steadfast belief that my poems would find a place in the world.

Thank you, Scott Owens, for sharing your love of poetry and for teaching the craft to so many so well. I am grateful for your encouragement in providing all of us aspiring poets with a beautiful place to be seen and heard at Poetry Hickory.

Thank you, Adrian Rice for your inspiration in class and constant poetry presence online. You make me think. (No higher professor compliment, right?)

Thank you, Terry, my first reader. You help me keep the wonder.

Credits to the following:

Wild Goose Poetry Review "World Series 1966"

Caldwell Arts Council, *Branches* "World Series 1966"

"Night Ride"

CVCC *Sanctuary Literary Journal* "I Always Bow My Head in that Sacred Silence"

"Conferring the Degree"

"Nature Knows What to Do"

Carolina Woman Magazine "Nature Knows What To Do"

Spitball Magazine "A Baseball Poem"

"End of the Season"

The News-Topic "Daylilies"

About the Author

Arlene Neal grew up in northern Stokes County, NC, in the tobacco farming community of Lawsonville on the NC/VA state line situated on a ridge between the Blue Ridge Mountains in Virginia to the north and the Sauratown Mountains to the south. Red clay soil, woods, fields, creeks, and the Dan River are in her DNA. Labeled Renaissance Woman by former students, Arlene Neal holds a bachelor's degree in biology and a master's in English Education from Appalachian State University. In retirement from Catawba Valley Community College English Department, she pursues poetry and continues to write a weekly column for the News-Topic of Lenoir, NC. She enjoys her large family, backyard bonfires, Sunday dinners, gardening, canning, birdwatching, reading, hiking, the Atlanta Braves, book clubs, and painting every now and then. She lives in the Dudley Shoals community of Caldwell County with her fisherman-husband Terry Neal who shares her faith journey.

www.ingramcontent.com/pod-product-compliance
Lightning Source LLC
Chambersburg PA
CBHW031210090426
42736CB00009B/860